Welcome to the Crazyverse

To Maisie
Hope you enjoy
the poems

Keith S...

Also by Keith Sheppard

Wonderland Revisited and the Games Alice Played There
(Evertype 2009)

Welcome to the Crazyverse

A collection of comic poems about famous people in history

by **Keith Sheppard**

Illustrations by
Kern Stewart

evertype

2012

Published by Evertype, Cnoc Sceichín, Leac an Anfa, Cathair na Mart, Co. Mhaigh Eo, Éire. *www.evertype.com*.

First edition 2012.

A catalogue record for this book is available from the British Library.

ISBN-10 1-904808-85-9
ISBN-13 978-1-904808-85-5

Typeset in Arno Pro and **Mikadan** by Michael Everson.

Illustrations: Kern Stewart

Cover: Michael Everson.

Printed by LightningSource.

Foreword

Funny thing, history—at least, it can be. Amazingly, some people still think history is boring. That's despite all the gory deaths, romance, intrigue, and people shooting at each other.

This collection of poems is loosely based on famous historical characters. Poems they may be, but not "poetry". This is comedy in verse.

Some are pure fantasy—it's unlikely Julius Caesar did his own grocery shopping, but where real events are mentioned, the facts are historically accurate.

For instance, any history student who commits *The Amorous Adventures of Good King Henry* to memory will know the names of all Henry VIII's wives, in the correct order, and how each met her end.

What was the real story behind the gunpowder plot (and who was this guy called Fawkes)? What happened after the English Civil War? How did Rasputin meet a sticky end? All these questions and more are answered in this book.

So forget those boring history lessons. Let's have a bit of fun together but beware. You may accidentally learn some history on the way…

To Jenny for putting up with me writing
when I really should have been getting on with life,
and for her encouragement in converting
this mere twinkle in my eye into a published book.

Contents

George and the Dragon

Since the dawning of time, man has always
        ignored
All the recommendations of vets,
And in efforts to stop himself getting too bored,
He has kept most unsuitable pets.

Such as lions and tigers, or even brown bears,
Who, to put it quite mildly, are pests.
They cover your carpets and curtains with hairs,
And have even been known to eat guests!

Yes the problems of feeding could fill up a tome,
And are almost too awful to tell.
Having eaten you right out of house and of
        home,
They can then eat you in it as well.

A really bad case happened long, long ago,
Just a couple of hundred A.D.
When a young English man found an egg in the
        snow
And decided to have it for tea.

Not an ordinary egg, mark you, no not at all,
It was green and it weighed half a pound.
If you stood it on end it was eight inches tall,
And it bounced if it dropped on the ground.

He filled up his wife's best and biggest cook pot.
He built up the fire in the grate.
Then leaving the water to get nice and hot,
He went off in search of a plate.

It didn't take long, he was back in a flash,
And although he was quite fit and able
He wasn't quite quick enough to save the crash
As the egg rolled and fell off the table.

It bounced on the floor and rose high in the air.
It must have been two feet or higher.
The egg bounced again, knocking over a chair,
Then it fell with a crash in the fire.

Now there's many might think (as indeed did the
        man)
This would mean nothing more than at most,
A minor adjustment to his dinner plan,
And instead of a boiled egg, eat roast.

But enveloped by flame the egg, bouncing no
        more,
Turned bright pink and then puce and then
        black.
Then emitting a sound like a rumbling roar
The egg shell proceeded to crack.

The shell cracked again, then it broke into two,
Revealing a perfect minute
Baby dragon cub, shiny and lively and new,
And looking exceedingly cute.

Straight away, he adored it, swore he'd tend it
       with pride,
That he'd feed it on mustard and chilli.
That he'd teach it to only breath fire when
       outside.
Even gave it a name—called it Billy.

The tragedy is that a dragon, of course,
Doesn't stay small and cute, that's for sure.
In a matter of weeks it's as big as a horse.
And it's fifty feet long when mature.

It was only six months till it outgrew the house
And it had to be kept in the barn.
"I think that is best," said his long-suffering
        spouse
"I am sure that he'll come to no harm."

But alas she was wrong, for the barn was too cold,
And the dragon developed a chill,
And maybe because it was not very old
It rapidly grew very ill.

It was while he was nursing it, though it was
        tame,
There occurred quite a major disaster.
The poor creature sneezed, shot a fountain of
        flame
That engulfed his unfortunate master.

The subsequent fire burned the barn to the
ground:
Just a pile of ash left where it stood.
The dragon meanwhile, with its freedom new
found,
Had escaped to a neighbouring wood.

For the next fifteen years 'twas the scourge of the
        town.
Fully grown, it turned mean and ferocious.
It would fly through the air and then swoop to
        the ground.
What it did then was really atrocious.

It would swallow a man in a single great gulp,
And it ate two or three every week.
A young boy or girl it would grind to a pulp
And then store them, for snacks, in its cheek.

As you can imagine, the folks from round there,
Were getting a little bit cross.
"We urgently need," they said, "someone who'll
        dare
To show this foul creature who's boss."

There were several brave but misguided young
        men
Who tried after a dragon attack
To follow it to its arboreal lair,
But none of them ever came back.

Until, that was, late on a warm summer's day
In the midst of a flaming July,
When a young English knight (who'd by chance
        lost his way)
Just happened to be passing by.

Desirous of somewhere to lay down his head,
And in need of some supper as well,
He broke up his journey by taking a bed
For the night at the local hotel.

When supper was over, this sociable knight
Decided to have half a jar
And to chat to the locals, as anyone might,
When alone in a strange hotel bar.

This was, of course, how the young nobleman
    learned
Of the monster that lived in the wood,
And just how many souls it had eaten or burned,
Every one of them honest and good.

Some may call him courageous, some may dub
       him a fool,
But that night he made this solemn vow—
He would end this foul dragon's tyrannical rule,
Though he didn't, just yet, know quite how.

Though I'm sure you'll have guessed, I shall tell
       you the name
Of this friendly young knight drinking beers.
It was George, and his destiny was that his fame
Would continue for years upon years.

George worked out his plan later on, in the bath.
It required only modest resources
Like a coil of stout rope plus a nice juicy half
Side of beef, and a couple of horses.

The villagers spent all the following morn
(Whilst Sir George had a lie-in, and rested)
Gathering up in a pile on the hotel's front lawn
The equipment that he had requested.

Then they all broke for lunch, save for one poor
young guy
Left defending the half side of beef
From a large pack of dogs, which had gathered
nearby,
And were drooling and gnashing their teeth.

After taking free lunch as the inn-keeper's guest
(A banquet of four or five courses)
The time came for George to depart on his quest,
So he saddled up both of his horses.

Then riding on one, and employing its friend
As a bearer for all of his gear,
He set off to, once and for all, put an end
To the fierce dragon's long reign of fear.

The wood, which the dragon had picked for its
                        lair,
Was only a few minutes ride,
So it wasn't too long till our hero was there
And had started to venture inside.

All was quiet and still in the shade of the trees
As Sir George commenced hunting around
Till the silence was rent by a roar fit to freeze
Up the blood, but Sir George stood his ground.

Just a couple of feet, right in front of the knight,
A large and quite dense holly bush
At that moment gave brave young Sir George
          quite a fright
By exploding in flames with a whoosh!

When the flames died away the poor bush was no
more,
And instead, standing there in its place,
Was the famous fierce dragon, with what Sir
George swore
Was a look of pure greed on its face.

George knew that he hadn't a moment to lose
Before setting in motion his plan,
Which relied on the hope that a dragon would
choose
To eat beefsteak in preference to man.

Restraining his horses' first instincts to leave,
Sir George quickly unsaddled the meat,
And with an almighty and strenuous heave
Made it land at the shocked dragon's feet.

Now a dragon's by no means the world's
        brightest beast,
Yet they say that its memory's not bad,
So this offering of such a splendid free feast
Stirred up memories of when 'twas a lad.

It had always remembered that humans and food
Were connected in some subtle way,
But forgetting just how, had been forced to
        conclude
That one ate one for lunch every day.

But now it recalled what it knew when a cub,
That the eating of men didn't pay.
Treat a man as your friend, and he still gave you
        grub,
But he lasted much longer that way.

So once it had got this magnificent feast
Of Sir George's prime beefsteak inside him,
The dragon was changed to a calm placid beast
That allowed George to saddle and ride him.

The dragon's two powerful wings then unfurled
And lazily started to flap,
Lifting dragon and rider both high 'bove the
        world,
Which was laid out beneath like a map.

Then using, as bridle, his stout coil of rope,
Sir George gently steered his mount to
A place where he thought they'd resources to
        cope
With a dragon—a neighbouring zoo.

Well over the decades, such stories as these
Will inevitably get embellished,
To the point where there's some who would
        claim, if you please,
That the dragon, at George's hand, perished.

While other folk, would you believe, have seen fit
To add a fair maid in distress,
Believing the story's in need of a bit
Of what they call "love interest".

But the truth of the matter, as you all now know,
Is such tales are mere fanciful writing.
Sir George just persuaded the dragon to go,
Without any bloodshed or fighting.

There's a moral to this little cautionary yarn—
To avoid any trouble and strife
Don't you try to keep wild creatures locked in
        your barn,
And be kind to all nature's wild life.

Julius Caesar and the Grocer

The emperor Julius Caesar and my Uncle
    Ebenezer,
So my uncle says, were really best of friends.
Was my uncle rich? Well, no sir.
He just ran the local grocer
Where the emperor often bought his odds and
    ends.
His assistant's name was Brutus, and would
    anyone dispute us
If we say one day when Jules was in the shop,
Brutus asked "Another fruit, eh?"
Answered Jules "I've ate two Brute,
So I really think it's time for me to stop."

Boadicea,
Queen of the Icy Knees

Boadicea was a lady
One would normally avoid,
And most certainly was not the sort
You'd like to get annoyed.

So the elders and advisors
On her council didn't dare
To say that in her chariot
She ought to take more care.

When she went driving down the street,
The people they all scattered
(For they knew that those who didn't
Were quite likely to get splattered).

Yes, the standard of her driving
Left a lot to be desired,
But anyone who told her
Ran the risk of being fired.

And I don't just mean they lost their job,
I mean they would be shot
From a special purpose catapult
This fearsome queen had got.

This dreadful situation
Carried on for many a year
Till a bright spark on her council
Had a rather good idea.

"Instead of ticking off our queen,
Make use of her," he said.
"Let us ask her if, in battle,
She could ride out at our head.

"Instead of in our streets and towns,
We'll let her run amok
Amongst the opposition's troops
And give them all a shock.

"To add to the confusion,
To each wheel we'll fix a knife.
That's sure to make the enemy
Go running for his life.

"We'll have them running to and fro."
The councillor repeated.
"And if she can chop their legs in half,
Our enemy's de-feeted!"

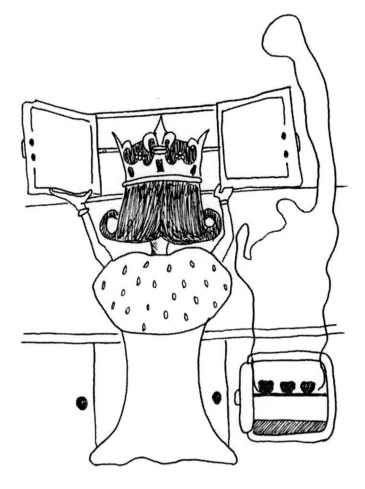

Alfred's Mistake

In days gone by, Alfred the Great,
Who made so few mistakes,
Searched too long to find a plate,
And thereby burned the cakes.

King William

William the First was nought but a boy
When he fractured his nose in a fight.
The senior physician in royal employ
Was told that he must put it right.

Well the good doctor bodged it, and so straight
      away
He went into hiding in terror.
And that's why the King ever after that day
Was always called "William the conk error".

The Ballad of Robin Hood

In days of old when knights were bold,
And baked beans weren't invented,
There lived a man in Nottingham,
And he was much resented.

The sheriff he, and plain to see
He didn't do it proper,
'Cause folks from there did oft declare
They wished he'd come a cropper.

Now in that land there was a band
Who gave the sheriff no rest.
These merry men had made their den
In depths of Sherwood Forest.

And at their helm, beneath the elm,
A man most highly thought of.
Yes in that wood lived Robin Hood
And was he brave? Well sort of.

Now in the week of which I speak
The sheriff, feeling naughty,
Hatched up a plan to catch this man,
And so prepared a sortie.

Our hero lad, a girl he had
With whom he liked to carry on.
An English rose with turned up nose
Who went by name of Marion.

The sheriff sent his best agent
To start this wicked chapter.
So at first light this evil knight
Embarked on Marion's capture.

At crack of dawn, across her lawn
He crept (there was no sentry).
Then up a drain and thus did gain
Himself illegal entry.

He searched and soon he'd found her room
And jumped Rob's would-be spouse.
Without a sound, he gagged and bound
And dragged her from the house.

Throughout that day the sheriff lay
Quite sound asleep in bed.
He knew in time news of his crime
Would surely start to spread.

He hoped that good young Robin Hood
Would hear, and think it best to
Round up his men, depart his glen
And try to stage a rescue.

Three days went past until at last
The sheriff cried "I see!
He hasn't dared. The man is scared.
He is no match for me.

"Lets plan anew, here's what we'll do.
(He'll fall for this of course.)
We'll tie his maid with lengths of braid
And plonk her on a horse.

"Then side by side, we two will ride
Beneath the Sherwood trees.
Just her and me, for all to see,
As brazen as you please.

"When he sees us, d'you think he'll suss
It is a trap? No not he.
He'll just guess that due to stress
I've gone a little potty.

"But he'll not know, my mortal foe,
The trick I have in mind.
He cannot harm me, 'cause my army
Follows on behind."

So after lunch, the sheriff's bunch
Were ready on their horses.
He with attractive female captive,
Followed by his forces.

Thus they did march past oak and larch
This man and captive frail.
While mighty hordes with bows and swords
Were following their trail.

'Twas just by luck, that friar Tuck
Was in the woods that day,
And chanced to fall to nature's call
In bushes by the way.

Concealed by briar, the jolly friar
Did Marion espy,
And the rotter who had got her
As they both rode by.

He stood aghast as they went passed.
He heard the sheriff's laughter.
He stood bog eyed as next he spied
The troops ten minutes after.

The chubby monk then did a bunk.
Leaped on his mule (called Dobbin),
And crossed the wood quick as he could
To tell his good friend Robin.

Now being an inventive man,
Rob hatched a cunning ruse
To foil the villain and, God willin',
Set his loved one loose.

Thus, Robin told four young men bold:
"Conceal the sheriff's track.
Each take a horse and tie some gorse
Securely to it's back.

"If then you go where e'er our foe
Has ridden, you will find
The prickly clumps tied to your rumps
Will smooth the trail behind."

To two men more he gave this chore:
"Go, take to horse and then
Please interpose between our foes
(The sheriff and his men).

"If this trick dupes the sheriff's troops
They'll follow you this day.
So please ensure they aren't a bore
By leading them astray."

The decoy trail, just couldn't fail.
The sheriff's troops elected
To track Rob's men through dale and glen,
As Robin had expected.

By tortuous track they led them back,
Delivering them with glee
Just like a parcel, to their castle—
Home in time for tea.

Our hero peerless, bold and fearless,
Used the intermission
To secrete that crack elite,
His hit-squad, in position.

He bade them hide on every side
Around a little clearing,
Which the portly sheriff shortly,
Rob thought, would be nearing.

He wasn't wrong, before too long
Old "Notts" was on the scene,
Looking like some fearsome pike,
All scaly, fat and mean.

Three paces more and then, for sure,
There could be no escaping.
Then with a shout, young Rob jumped out.
The sheriff just sat gaping.

"Unhand that wench, before my hench-
Men cut you to a shred.
Let go, I say, without delay."
Is what our hero said.

The sheriff vile said with a smile:
"I fear you are confounded.
For as we speak, you foolish freak,
My troops have your surrounded."

Replied our hero: "Dear, oh dear, no.
What you say's untrue.
My men adept did intercept
The army following you.

"Your troops aren't here. They're home I fear.
Their faces they are stuffin'.
Eating ham and bread with jam
And nice hot toasted muffin."

The sheriff frowned and stamped the ground
And looked quite circumspect.
He shouted: "Drat! You are a rat."
(Or words to that effect).

Then he swore and stamped some more,
And yelled till he was blue.
But Robin's plan had foiled the man.
There's nothing he could do.

And that my friends is how it ends.
Our hero's reunited
With his heart throb. Well done smart Rob!
Everyone's delighted.

There's just one more quite pleasant chore
That falls to me to do.
That's to relate the fitting fate
Befalling you-know-who.

The evil cad is hopping mad
For Robin had him bound
And held to ransom for the handsome
Sum of forty pound.

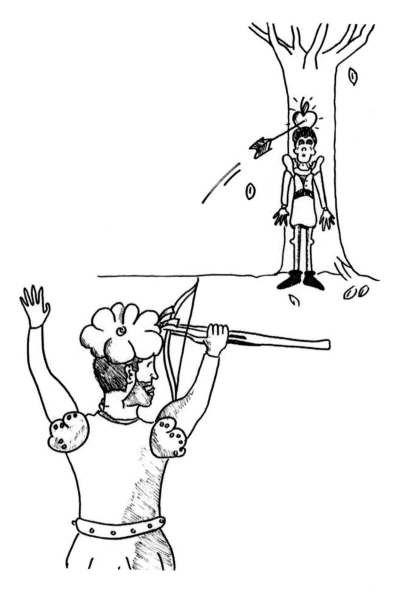

Guessler's Speech to William Tell

"Dead, dead! That's what I said,
If you can't hit that apple on your young son's
        head.

"My, my. Arrow fly.
Make sure that you're accurate, don't hit him in
        the eye.

"Tell, Tell, you've done too well.
You sent out your arrow and the apple fell.

"Oh no, mortal foe,
Now you've won my challenge I must let you
        go!"

Wars of the Roses

I really must ask you just what you suppose is
The reason why Englishmen fought over roses.

The people of Lancaster, so it is said,
Were really quite adamant, roses are red.

Whilst the good men of York said "By gum, that
        ain't right.
Surely everyone knows that a rose should be
        white."

The simple solution, or so one might think,
Would be compromise and have a rose which is
        pink.

But the people in those days were really quite
        poor
At resolving such things without going to war.

So battle was joined and raged fearsome and long
As to which rose was right, and thus which one
was wrong.

Now I really would like to be able to say
That such trivial tiffs could not happen today.

But I only last week met a young Texan fellow
Who told me quite forcefully "roses are yellow."

Vlad the Impaler

There once was a tyrant named Vlad.
An unusual habit he had.
Those who earned his dislike
He impaled on a spike
(He was really a little bit mad).

The Amorous Adventures of Good King Henry

Henry the Eighth, a fickle king,
Couldn't make up his mind
Whether he should take a wife,
And, if so, just what kind.

He first chose brother Arthur's wife
(Poor Art had, sadly, died)
One Catherine of Aragon
To be his queen and bride.

Now it was Henry's dearest wish
To have a son and heir.
But though she tried, his trusty wife
Just could not help him there.

Of several babes, just one survived,
But not a little boy.
The little princess Mary was
Their only scrap of joy.

This made the King feel most fed up.
He blamed it on his wife.
Convinced she was responsible
For all this pain and strife.

A young and nubile wench at court
Then led him into sin.
Who was this girl who bowled him o'er?
Well it was Anne Boleyn.

To take his mistress as his wife,
The King saw just one course.
Although it narked the church of Rome,
He underwent divorce.

His second marriage bore as fruit
Another young princess.
This one they named Elizabeth
(For short, they called her Bess).

Still Henry wasn't satisfied,
And soon began believing
A wife so young and beautiful
Must surely be deceiving.

He thought that every knave at court
Was wooing her to bed,
And so cut short his time with her
By chopping off her head.

He straightway married Jane Seymour—
At last he had a boy,
But poor old Jane died giving birth,
So sadness tempered joy.

His next wife was the brainchild
Of a scheming politician:
A match designed to bring about
A national coalition.

A sister to the Duke of Cleves,
Her name was Anne of same.
But Henry hated her straight-way
When to his court she came.

Bad luck for her selector, Cromwell,
It cost him his life.
And for the King, a quick divorce
To rid him of this wife.

Again the naughty fruity King
By passion was devoured
For another young nymphet.
This one was Catherine Howard.

Alas this girl was not content
To be the King's consort.
She played around with anyone
That way inclined at court.

This was a silly thing to do,
It cannot be disputed,
Because, of course, the King found out
And had her executed.

'Twas only then that finally
He changed his restless ways,
And with his last wife, Catherine Parr,
He did live out his days.

Sir Walter Raleigh

Sir Walter Raleigh, a really good bloke
(He even let Queen Lizzie stand on his cloak),
Did but one foolish thing, and it's really no joke,
He imported tobacco and taught us to smoke.

Armada!
(Actually, it was *their* Mada)

In fifteen eighty eight the fleet
Of Spanish Philip tried to beat
The English and effect invasion.
I'm pleased to say, on this occasion,
England was too well defended.
Poor old Philip's plans were ended
By such folk as Francis Drake,
Whose very name forced foes to quake
And Frobisher and Hawkins too,
Though less well known to me and you,
All played their part that fateful day
When Philip's ships were sent away.
I guess, however, most of all
They were defeated by a squall.
A sudden wind of such great force
It blew the Spanish ships off course,
Thus prompting Lizzie One to say
That God had blown them clean away.

Gunpowder, Treason, and Plot

My story begins quite a long time ago
In the springtime of sixteen-oh-five,
When some angry young men vowed the King
        had to go,
They could no longer bear him alive.

The reason that tempers were running so hot
Amongst some of King James' minions
Was that he and a few of his subjects had got
Wildly different religious opinions.

The King was a protestant man through and
        through,
And he drove all the Catholics mad,
For his treatment of such folk, between me and
        you,
Was really a little bit bad.

The leading dissenter was one Robert Catesby.
His friends gathered round him and cried:
"We agree James must go, so how long must the
     wait be?"
So Catesby stood up and replied...

"Oh please do remember the fifth of November,
For that's when the evil King James
With his parliament sits. We shall blow them to
     bits.
We shall send the whole lot up in flames.

"It's a gem of a plan, but there's danger, that's
     why
It's essential that nobody talks.
And a gunpowder expert is needed, so I
Have recruited some guy they call Fawkes."

So Catesby and his group of like minded fellahs,
Who all bore the King the same malice,
Put their plan into action by renting some cellars
Which ran under Westminster Palace.

Then into this pit the conspirators stowed
Quite a number of barrels of powder.
It was more than enough so that, should it
            explode,
As bangs go, there are few would be louder.

Then, for the duration of summer recess,
The gunpowder plotters dispersed,
Believing the start of November was best
For powder kegs doing their worst.

It was whilst the assassins were biding their time
Till parliament next was in session,
That one of their number committed the crime
Of careless unwise indiscretion.

It seems Francis Tresham's own brother in law
Was a member of parliament so
Of course Frankie warned him "My lord, I
        implore,
When the house reconvenes, please don't go.

"I hope you won't think that there's something
        awry,
It's just that I think that it's best
If you let the first day of the session go by.
You look tired and in need of a rest."

Young Frankie's relation, by name Lord
        Monteagle,
I'm sorry to say, smelt a rat.
"I'm sure," he said, "Frank's up to something
        illegal,
Else why should he speak out like that?"

Suspicions thus roused, on the eve of the day
That parliament met once again,
A search of the buildings was put under way
By some of King James' best men.

They searched and they searched to see what
        could be found.
They searched the whole place top to bottom.
If only they'd done it the other way round,
Then much quicker would they have got 'em.

For down in the cellars, amongst all the rats,
Was where the King's men apprehended
The unfortunate Fawkes and his gunpowder vats,
With which the King's life could be ended.

In those days, of course, people had no idea
Of a criminal's right to be silent.
Their questioning methods were sometimes,
                I fear,
A little bit gruesome and violent.

And so it is only a matter of time
Before our friend Guy Fawkes confesses,
Revealing the nature of his would-be crime
And accomplices names and addresses.

So that was the end of the violent schemes
Of Catesby and Winter and Wright
And others whose mark on our history, it seems,
Was giving us bonfire night.

So please do remember the fifth of November,
Gunpowder, treason and plot,
When the guy they called Guy tried to blow them
      sky high,
All that parliamentarian lot.

The World's First Superstar

Sixteen hundred and forty nine
Was not a very good year
To be a king of England
Or a royal prince, I fear.

For then it was that Charlie One
Was severed from his head.
The puritans had triumphed and
The monarchy was dead.

To save his hide, his son and heir
Was forced to flee the nation
And book himself, in sunny France,
An extra long vacation.

Alas it really isn't fun
To be an exiled king,
A stranger in that foreign land
Where bread is long and thin.

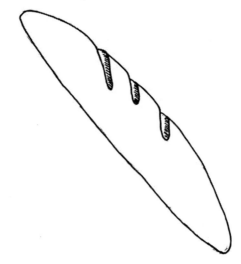

Away from all your folks and friends
And forced to live among
A race who think frogs' legs are food
And speak a foreign tongue.

So thus it was the young Prince Charles
Was forced to find his own
Amusements which, regrettably
Were of low moral tone.

His favourite way to pass the time
Was with a pretty wench
Who he'd impress with regal airs,
Then chat her up in French.

Meanwhile back in his native land
Began a change of fad,
As some declared the monarchy
Was really not so bad.

You see, my friends, a puritan
Is the most frightful bore,
Believing everything that's fun
Should be against the law.

They shut down all the theatres,
Clamped down on dance and song.
That's not a situation which
Could be endured for long.

They stuck it out eleven years,
But then the English nation,
Deciding that they'd had enough
Embarked on restoration.

So Charles returned from exile to
A welcome truly royal
And subjects who all promised him
"We henceforth shall be loyal.

"We know we hunted down your dad,
And when we caught our quarry,
We went and chopped his head off, well
We now are truly sorry."

So Charles forgave them every one.
(Well what choice had he got?
He couldn't execute them all
And get another lot.)

Now whilst all this was going on,
In a back street London pub,
There was a comely wench whose job
Was serving drinks and grub.

Her mother ran this bawdy house.
Her dad had died a debtor,
And this young lass, named Nelly Gwynn,
Was sure she could do better.

It was her elder sister, Rose,
Suggested to our Nell,
That oranges in Drury Lane
Would, very likely, sell.

"I reckon, Sis, you could do well.
Just choose a decent pitch.
That theatre crowd's a hungry lot,
And most of them are rich."

Now Nelly was the sort of girl
Whose fortune was her face.
The sort who's irresistible
When bonny-donned in lace.

A lot of theatre people have
An eye for nature's art,
And one such individual
Was thespian Charlie Hart.

He met our Nell one fateful night
When out in Drury Lane
And instantly he saw in her
Potential wealth and fame.

He trained her in both dance and song,
And in dramatic art.
Before too long he found for her
Her very first stage part.

Well Nelly was, without a doubt,
An overnight sensation,
Who captured nearly every heart
Within the British nation.

Every play that Nell was in
Was sell-out from first night.
No high-class party was complete
Without Nell Gwynn's invite.

And if a late-night chat-show host
Was looking for the best,
Then little pretty witty Nell
Just had to be his guest.

So great was Nelly's fame she even
Met the King one night,
And though it sounds quite corny it
Was love upon first sight.

Although the King was married, he
Still liked a pretty girl.
With Nelly it was more than that—
She made the King's heart twirl.

He gave her dresses, diamonds, pearls,
The best that could be bought,
A splendid house with servants, and
Presented her at court.

The King's largess extended even
To Nell Gwynn's old mum,
Who got a house in Chelsea, worth
An astronomic sum.

Our Nelly was extravagant.
'Twas well the King adored her.
It took a man of royal means
To manage to afford her.

The British public worshipped her.
Like movie stars today,
Her perfect looks and lavish style
Inspired them in some way.

It did not matter that she was
A mistress to the King,
For in those days they made less fuss
About that sort of thing.

And even on his death-bed, Charles
Was heard to weakly say
"Let not poor Nelly starve" before
He quietly passed away.

His brother and successor, James,
Thus took it on himself
To see his brother's mistress never
Pined through lack of wealth.

And so, my friends, should you be asked
Who you think could have been
The first show-business superstar
The world has ever seen.

Was it Shirley Temple Black
When she was just a child?
Charlie Chaplin, Lillian Gish,
Or even Oscar Wilde?

You can answer "None of those
'Twas earlier by far.
Think back to Stuart England,
And to Nell Gwynn, superstar."

Beethoven

Beethoven, Ludwig van
Was a truly exceptional man.
Whilst as deaf as a post
He wrote some of the most
Brilliant music (of which I'm a fan).

On the Subject of Kings

This evening I've been studying
To try to learn some history,
But still there are some aspects
Which are something of a mystery.

My friends all say it's easy,
That there's really nothing to it,
That William was a Norman,
And Charlie was a Stuart,

But I can't see the logic,
Though I've tried with all my might.
I don't see why these silly kings
Can't get their first names right.

On the Subject of Artists

It is really very queer
Why Van Gogh cut off his ear
And Picasso always painted things in blues,
Why Da Vinci's Mona Lisa
Looks like not a thing could please her
And that man Lautrecht just had to have two
      loos.

Ode to the Model T Ford

Henry Ford was never bored
And goodness gracious me,
He had the art of the horseless cart
Perfected to a T.

The Untimely Demise of Grigori Rasputin

There is really no disputin'
That when Grigori Rasputin
Met the Russian Queen, his heart was set aflame,
But it wasn't for the lady,
For this monk was rather shady,
And desired power, influence and fame.

Now Rasputin was quite clever,
So it didn't take forever
Till the Queen was well and truly in his spell.
For he made himself alluring
By a clever feat of curing
When he made young Prince Alexei fit and well.

This made the Queen so grateful
That she took the sly and hateful
Monk to be her close advisor and her friend.
But he abused this post of power,
Plotting each and every hour,
Trying to turn affairs of state to his own ends.

Thus Rasputin was much hated
And was consequently fated
To fall victim to assassins, who had sworn
That the monk was just too awful
So, although it was unlawful,
They just could not let him see another dawn.

One of those who wished to pop off
This mad monk was Prince Yusopov
Who invited him around for wine and cake.
Well, he got the monk to dine
On some poisoned cake and wine
But, alas, it only made his stomach ache.

So the Prince, in panic, ran,
Got his gun and shot the man
But still the stubborn monk refused to die.
Then a friend named Vladimir
Cried "Yusopov, give him here.
I've got my gun, please let me have a try."

Thus the monk was shot again
But alas 'twas still in vain
For the spark of life was just not going to wither.
So they tried another tack—
Tied his hands behind his back
And then threw him, through the ice, into the
       river.

Now for those who seek a moral,
It is this: you should not quarrel
With your countrymen. Don't take, but be a
       giver.
For it isn't very nice
To be poisoned then shot twice
Then be drowned beneath an ice cold freezing
       river.

Morse Code
(With guide to pronunciation)

A	•—	Deedah	N	—•	Daddy
B	—•••	Daddy diddy	O	———	Dadah dah
C	—•—•	Daddy daddy	P	•——•	Deedah daddy
D	—••	Daddy dee	Q	——•—	Dadah deedah
E	•	Dee	R	•—•	Deedah dee
F	••—•	Diddy daddy	S	•••	Diddy dee
G	——•	Dadah dee	T	—	Dah
H	••••	Diddy diddy	U	••—	Diddy dah
I	••	Diddy	V	•••—	Diddy deedah
J	•———	Deedah dadah	W	•———	Deedah dah
K	—•—	Daddy dah	X	—••—	Daddy deedah
L	•—••	Deedah diddy	Y	—•——	Daddy dadah
M	——	Dadah	Z	——••	Dadah diddy

A Morse Ode

Poor Samuel Morse, he was feeling quite hoarse
And his voice wasn't working one day .
"Dadah dah," he exclaimed then a "diddy diddy!"
For that's all he was able to say.

"Diddy, diddy dee, deedah, daddy dadah!" he
      cried,
As he thought to himself in this mode.
I could add in here lots of new dashes and dots,
But there's quite enough code in this ode.

Relativity

Drei, zwei, eins, mein
Gott, Herr Einstein,
How did you figure it all out?
That light takes the same time
To travel in a straight line
Even when those watching move about.

If a light ray that you see
Moves as fast when viewed by me
Despite the fact I'm flying really fast
You deduced that in the end,
It is time itself must bend
Even though the thought left everyone aghast.

And although you might protest
You're on the bus when I'm at rest
And you think your watch not prone to running
    slow.
The effect is very small
Hardly anything at all
At the sort of speeds we humans tend to go.

But travel very fast
And you'll start to see at last
That the flow of time has slowed down to a crawl.
And, incredibly, you'll find
That the folk you left behind
Will have all grown old whilst you've not aged at
    all.

Though your theories seem quite odd
And like you're playing dice with God
In fact the universe is stranger than it seems.
For large masses make a dent
Meaning space itself gets bent
Putting kinks into the paths of all light beams.

Don't protest that it's not true
For I shall tell you, if you do,
That such things aren't merely theories any more.
Rocket science, electronics
GPS and nucleonics
All rely to some degree on Einstein's laws.

So you are my nummer eins, mein
Lieb' Professor Einstein,
You set the world of physics in a fizz.
For it is through your great insight
Into such things as space and light
That technology today is where it is.

War!

The Great War they called it then
But really it wasn't that great.
The war to end all wars they said
But sadly that wasn't its fate.

It may seem, at first, that it's not very much
Just an archduke, in Bosnia, shot.
Did it upset the balance in Europe a touch?
No. It upset the balance a lot.

For Austria-Hungary wanted a fight
And maintained that the Serbs were to blame.
The Russians then said "Nyet, nyet, nyet, that
            ain't right."
And so in on the Serbs' side they came.

A number of treaties then came into force
As nations joined in, one by one.
The Germans, the French and we Britons of
         course
We were all asked to pick up a gun.

The Great War they called it then
Because most of the world joined the fight.
The war to end all wars, they said
And it's really a shame they weren't right.

And so they did battle in air, sea and trench
For some four grim and wearisome years,
While soldiers dug in mid the rats, filth and
         stench
Facing death and disease, pain and fears.

They didn't call it World War One
Because no one expected a second.
The war to end all wars they said
But things didn't turn out how they reckoned.

For just two decades on, a new cause for alarm
Were the Nazis, with Hitler their head.
PM Chamberlain went there to try talk some
      calm
And when he got back here he said:

"What I have in my hand is a small piece of paper
Promising peace in our time.
There won't be a war if we don't light the taper
'Cause Hitler and I got on fine."

But we all of us know now it wasn't too bright
To think Hitler a man to ignore,
For Adolf then marched into Poland to fight
And thus triggered another world war.

This time they called it World War Two,
Deciding it best to keep count,
For no one believed it the end of all wars
And the tally was starting to mount.

We have since had an era of relative peace.
Mind you, wars never quite go away.
Wishful thinking, perhaps, that they'd totally
      cease
But you never know… maybe one day.

A war to end of all wars, perhaps
Was a hope that was never to be.
But if you must fight then be vigilant, chaps,
Not to kick off world war number three.

Lightning Source UK Ltd.
Milton Keynes UK
UKOW050602240212

187876UK00001B/6/P

9 781904 808855